Starting from 'I Don't Know'

Starting from 'I Don't Know'

Interviews on Architecture and Craft

Samuel P. Smith

SOBERSCOVE PRESS

CHICAGO

SOBERSCOVE PRESS
www.soberscove.com

Starting from 'I Don't Know': Interviews on Architecture and Craft
© 2015 Samuel P. Smith

Starting from 'I Don't Know'–Workshop Studio Mumbai: Architecture between Experiment and Expertise by Samuel P. Smith was published in 2012 by ETH Zurich. Soberscove Press is grateful to ETH Zurich for permission to proceed with the present edition, a revised version of Smith's original publication.

Organizers of Workshop Studio Mumbai:
Sitterwerk: Ueli Vogt with Bijoy Jain and Felix Lehner; Zurich University of Applied Sciences, Winterthur: Hubert Mäder; Lucerne University of Applied Sciences and Arts: Sebastian Holzhausen and Hannes Zweifel; ETH Zurich: Gian Salis.

Organizers of the exhibition *Work-Place Studio Mumbai*:
Ueli Vogt and Bijoy Jain with Sam Barclay, Katalin Deér, Lukas Furrer, Fabio Hunziker, Louisa Keel, Felix Lehner, Johann Reble, Ariane Roth, Marina Schütz, and Thomas Stüssi.

All interviews (with the exception of the Bijoy Jain interview) were translated from the original German by Samuel P. Smith.

Image credits:
p. 2 © 2011 Lorenz Bachmann
pp. 6, 15, 28, 32, 38, 42, 49, 55, 56, 60, 67 © 2011 Gian Salis
pp. 10, 11, 12, 16, 24, 31, 36, 37, 45, 46, 50, 68, 69 © 2011 Katalin Deér
p. 56 © 2011 Marco Ganz

Available through ARTBOOK | D.A.P
75 Broad Street, Suite 630
New York, NY 10004
www.artbook.com

ISBN: 978-1-940190-07-5
Second Printing 2019
Design by Rita Lascaro
Cover photograph by Katalin Deér

Contents

Introduction

In a moment of idle curiosity after submitting my architectural degree project in Zurich, I signed up for a weeklong workshop with Bijoy Jain, founder of Studio Mumbai. With images in my mind of the tools and artifacts exhibited by Studio Mumbai in the Arsenale during the 2010 Venice Biennale, I arrived at Sitterwerk in St. Gallen, Switzerland, one morning in July 2011. Other expectant architecture students had come as well, together with craftspeople, artists, and architects. As it turned out, no one really knew what was going to happen.

Bijoy started out by having us mix fire clay, a waste product from the art foundry at Sitterwerk, with plaster and water. Without a defined goal in mind, we followed his instructions about how to build up layer after layer with a trowel; for many of us, this direct act of making was a novel experience.

Bijoy brought with him not only a profound knowledge of materials and craft techniques, but also facility for letting questions of design and execution flow together in a search for interesting solutions. According to Bijoy's way of working, you tickle out the conceptual and technical potential of any available material substance through experimentation. What is "forbidden" becomes merely untried; errors and conflicting results have the potential to develop into new techniques and expressions. All the while, deep and focused observation guides the growth of understanding.

There could not, perhaps, be a more fitting place than Sitterwerk to host this kind of inquiry. A complex of various artistic and cultural enterprises, it populates a former industrial site along the Sitter River and celebrates the chance encounters facilitated by the close proximity of its sculpture foundry, materials archive, art library, gallery, and artists' studios.

Among the workshop's stream of material experimentation, demonstrations of craft techniques, and discussions in a mix of languages, the factual knowledge about construction and building materials that I had learned in my architecture school's lectures slowly began to lose its firmness. A different type of knowledge was softening it: the wisdom and know-how of the master craftsperson, which can only develop through countless hours of physical contact with a material and observation of its behavior in many situations.

At the end of the workshop, Katalin Deér, one of the organizers and a participating artist, suggested that I put together some sort of documentation. Composed of interviews with several participants (as well as photographs and recipes), the original version of *Starting from 'I Don't Know'* was primarily intended for the participants of the workshop and its sponsoring institutions; no great attempt was made to reach a wider audience. However, two years after the workshop, Julia Klein discovered the book during an artist's residency in the Sitterwerk library and proposed distributing it through her publishing house, Soberscove Press. This idea gradually evolved into a reworking of the book.

Of course, this project depended on many people. I am grateful to the participants of the workshop who allowed themselves be interviewed. Their observations and stories are the reason it has come into being. I was very fortunate to have Lecturer Gian Salis as my advisor; his astuteness gave my exploration focus. I am also deeply indebted to Professor Annette Spiro of the ETH Zurich Department of Architecture, for sponsoring the publication of the first version of *Starting from 'I Don't Know'* as an independent elective project. Most importantly, my gratitude goes to Bijoy Jain, for sharing his time so generously with all of us.

Katalin Deér has played a vital role in this project; I cannot thank her enough for her initial impulse to document the workshop and what her suggestion has set in motion. Furthermore, her numerous photographs captured the various episodes of the workshop beautifully, and became the atmospheric cornerstone of the experience's visual memory.

Samuel P. Smith
September 2015

Hubert Mäder

Be Fluid

It's only thanks to a coincidence that the Studio Mumbai Workshop took place at Sitterwerk in St. Gallen.
Yes. I had invited Bijoy Jain to give a lecture at the architecture school in Winterthur in November 2010, but he appeared a day early, so we spontaneously visited Sitterwerk. This special workplace, with its art foundry, art library, and material archive, greatly impressed Bijoy; in that combination he saw an approach similar to that of Studio Mumbai. Building on this kindred spirit, Ueli Vogt, then the director of the material archive, proposed to bring the exhibition *Work-Place Studio Mumbai* to Sitterwerk. In this context the workshop then became possible.

What originally interested you?
In the summer of 2010, Studio Mumbai caught my attention with the exhibition *Learning from Vernacular*, near Lausanne. Two short videos from the studio showed someone sitting cross-legged and working on a piece of wood, relaxed and unhurried. The architecture initially remained in the

background. Later, I realized that Studio Mumbai works with very large mock-ups and many model variants in a large workshop beneath the palm trees—there were rumors of 150 employees. When I saw the stylized photographs of the buildings, taken by Hélène Binet, it became clear to me that someone was operating with great focus there.

What makes the connection between craft and architecture so interesting?

Craft plays an important role in the realization of architecture. However, often our understanding of craft remains on a superficial level. We tend to underestimate how much craft depends on doing things over and over again and practicing them in constant repetition.

In our week together, we produced many material samples in a short period of time. It was important to experience that craft requires a certain humility. You have to realize that experts who are obsessed with their work have been advancing and perfecting their knowledge and skill over decades. It's up to us to tap into that knowledge.

How was this manifested in the workshop?

I came to the conclusion that we architects can acquire new ideas and knowledge when we engage with craft experts. In retrospect, however, I was also interested in asking myself what aspects are most important when dealing with craft: Is it the final surface, or the process of making, or is it ultimately only the cost? Or that it goes well for the craftsman? Should he suffer if he makes a mistake? Or is there not a greater

openness for other forms of collaboration? Bijoy said it
beautifully, "Be fluid."

Bijoy Jain

Starting from 'I Don't Know'

For our first experiment, you chose crushed fire clay, a waste product of the art foundry at Sitterwerk, the site of our workshop. Mixing it with plaster and water, we applied it onto a cement tile with a trowel. How does this characterize your way of working?

Coming into the workshop, I wasn't quite sure what the available materials were, so in a sense I was responding to the situation: walking onto a site and trying to make a connection. The clay was something we could physically use. I didn't know how to use it; Felix and Katalin's sense for that became local know-how and served as a basis for our engagement—observing small changes, gauging how thick a layer of plaster should be, and noting its physical color. I simulated something very close to how Studio Mumbai would approach a circumstance like this.

How do the concrete (the material) and the abstract (the concept) relate in your projects?

I think it is a combination of the two. A material exists in reality—has a color, a texture. The abstract would be my response to this physical material and what this physical material evokes within me—through memory, experience, my dreams. The combination results in an oscillation between the two. If I reverse that and think abstractly, what is then abstract produces a concrete response. The movement between the concrete and the abstract is a continuous process of discovery, within myself, but also within the material, and both are interdependent. The resulting reality connects you to memory: what is there now, or a future possibility. It can capture different points of view, different times; it goes beyond the physical limitations of just being there. That's how I understand the concrete and the abstract, just purely through the investigation of the material.

You always begin with the concrete, the material?
Not necessarily, it can even just be a random thought, or the random act of cutting the ground, which then triggers an engagement with the material. Palmyra House, for example, began with the idea of very light, suspended lanterns in the palm grove. At first we designed it with highly polished concrete walls, fifteen centimeters thick, cast in a graphite color so they would reflect the landscape. I didn't know how to engineer concrete at that point, so I had to rely on an engineer, who specified a thickness close to thirty centimeters, and then the entire idea of the project somehow was lost. I realized that I could not rely on an outside source, but only on the skills of those around me.

Through the process of chasing that emotional quality of the idea of illumination, we slowly moved to timber. The project developed, the materials developed, but whatever we did was registered against the abstract idea of these glowing lanterns.

How much do the craftspeople contribute to conceptual discourse?
Let me give you an example. During the monsoon, we were surveying a project where basically the central portion of this particular piece of land fills up with water. You cannot physically occupy the space, even though the water level goes down in the dry season. Six of us were rocking in this little canoe, trying to keep it from tipping over, and Jeevaram, who is my head carpenter, was very specific in how he would take a position in that space and he described his idea of the structure. That's a conceptual discussion, so then it's my turn to respond.

On another project, I was physically away from the studio and three of the younger carpenters developed the project from their own sensibilities. I did a little sketch and they took it a little further—not the way I would do it, but similar.

I'm curious about making a sound and getting a response. It may be different from what you expected, and bit-by-bit you adjust. It's like free jazz: with experience you begin to understand the nuances, a certain communication transpires from playing together.

Everyone improvises then?
We share the spiritual belief that everyone participates. There

are moments, however, when I have to call the shots, like the driver of a car who is ultimately responsible for the trip. In our studio we set up a framework, but how everyone responds to that framework is an open discussion. Even my wife Priya gets involved, and she's not an architect. Once we had to decide on a specific material and Jeevaram and other senior craftspeople, even Priya, unanimously favored the opposite of my opinion. For the previous six months I had been aligned with what they were saying, but that day it was exactly the opposite. I was struggling with not having much control, but by instinct alone, I agreed to the others' views and started working from their standpoint. I was then able to bring up what had been troubling me. They acknowledged my concern and we immediately came up with something that was better than any of the previous options. By accepting dissonance, we combined many points into a broader view, like an open fan. This relates the project more universally to human experience.

Some craftspeople continue a family tradition into the fortieth generation. How does this influence the interplay between thinking and making?
That's an interesting question. Jeevaram, the head carpenter, started apprenticing at twelve. He said that even though he was surrounded by traditional techniques, never once did he pay attention to all the stuff happening around him. He was more interested in novel processes like gluing veneers on plywood or using materials like Styrofoam. He never realized that all of the traditional things that surrounded him would end up shaping the skills he is using today.

The craftspeople here, I believe, have access to what they saw and experienced as children. When they are working or drawing now, they can dive into the space of their memories, like diving into a sea of experience, where they can find a response for developing an idea or defining a construction detail. I'm not quite sure; I think that's what they do.

There is also a form of collective memory, a knowledge that inhabits physical things and transmits itself in a process of osmosis between artisan and artifact. For instance, in the workshop, Ruedi Krebs talked about this piece of stone floor from a medieval church that he had to redo; the original craftsperson had of course long passed away, so Ruedi had to go through the process of learning directly from this piece of stone how the floor had been made, and how he would have to repair it.

How did it come about that you and Ruedi Krebs did a full-scale wall mock-up together? Was it different from your experiences in India?
The question had come up as to how I would work in Switzerland. A dinner conversation with Ruedi sparked the idea of the mock-up, and I made a sketch. That started the dialogue with Ruedi and then from there, you know, one doesn't know where it will lead. One of the carpenters at Sitterwerk built the frame, we put in the slats, and then we plastered it with clay around the wooden joints and then lime. My interest oscillated between what I wanted to do and discovering the material that Ruedi had talked about.

Within the confines of the workshop, this collaboration was brief. Do you depend on long-term collaboration within Studio Mumbai?

It depends; sometimes too familiar is not good, because it doesn't lead to unpredictability. I like to keep the idea of freshness, so while you gain experience, maintaining naiveté or openness is also important, like when you were a kid, or a first-year student in architecture school. This freshness has a lifespan, but it can also go on forever, always moving. You expand your knowledge and at the same time you are able to come in with no knowledge. We work toward this spirit in Studio Mumbai, an open creativity that extends much further than the group itself.

Extending to your clients as well?

Yes and no; I think it's demanding to expect that from a client. The reason we started doing mock-ups was to make our intent transparent to the client. Sometimes they engage, sometimes they don't, but it's a way to make them curious. On one project, the clients really weren't connected to the plans and drawings in front of them, so I invited them to the site, where we did a full-scale mock-up of the whole house with cheap wood slats and screen, and served them tea there. They began evaluating the sizes of the rooms, and through that they finally engaged.

We take for granted that everybody sees architecture the way we see it. But I don't know how to read music, and if a musician put a piece of musical writing in front of me, I wouldn't be able to make any sense of it. It would have to be played for it to make sense to me. It's the responsibility of the architect to make a connection to the client. It's not about education, but communication. By using such methods, you disempower the resistance of not knowing.

What resistance did you encounter in the workshop?
Things like, "Oh, in Switzerland we can't do this, we can't do that." I don't believe that's true; anything is possible, but you have to engage. Architecture is more complex than just making buildings. Emotions, memories, food, etc., are all possible beginning points for architecture. That's how I like to produce architecture; it keeps me on different journeys that are unexpected. Being curious is very important, and not worrying about how I am going to do it. Rather: Let's explore, let's see, let's find out.

Ruedi Krebs

Involved Too Late

Over the course of decades you've rediscovered the techniques of building with lime and have given these techniques new recognition. How do you see yourself today?

We craftspeople are in a very tricky situation because we are involved much too late. When planners find themselves in trouble, they call us up and maybe we'll be able to fix the issue. We're not allowed to contribute our thoughts and knowledge early enough. Architects often think in terms of industrial product systems, but I'm not interested in answering to these industrial products when I'm called in for construction. My craft can think in its own terms, has its own approach, and also wants an expression of its own. I always regret that we're too far removed from the development of ideas.

So you see yourself in conflict with industry?

I don't want to be a product assembler! You no longer go to a carpenter who creates a bed for you. You go to a designer who creates a bed for thousands. Craft has been stripped of its true scope of work, pushed aside by industry. That your material has ten thousand years of experience doesn't count anymore, it seems. There are so many salespeople trying to sell you the latest novelty.

This condition had already advanced to the point where there was no more living knowledge about building with limestone.

I could not apprentice with someone to learn what I do. However, craft depends on observing others and practicing, like music. Through practice you learn that there are certain laws about how you can construct something. You also learn how to use your body, how to find a rhythm. Many of these things were never written down, the passing down of knowledge was interrupted. That's also why limestone is surrounded by so much myth: should it be stored for three, or five, or ten years?

Tell me about the wall mock-up you produced with Bijoy and the Sitterwerk carpenter. Was that a familiar way of working?

I thought it was very good that we simulated the process the way it would happen in his studio. I understood exactly what he was after in that sketch of a wooden frame that he did. With the carpenter, who unfortunately was not present from the beginning, we made those frames, and I proposed putting in slats. One also could have used some branches, a familiar technique. I had actually wanted to find out how they deal with softwood in India, but apparently they don't know about it there, because it doesn't grow in the tropical climate. And we use it for building! For me, the interesting thing was playing through all of the possibilities.

Returning to your regret about coming in too late as a craftsperson: what problems arise out of this situation?
As an architect, you can only think along the lines of what you've already experienced. If you've never experienced limestone, you won't think of limestone. The lively ones are an exception to this, and Bijoy showed very clearly how he expands the scope of his investigation by letting things emerge, not yet knowing where everything will lead. When a standard architecture office comes to a craftsperson, they already know what they want and nothing new can be created. In such cases, I think architecture limits its true range of expression.

Katalin Deér

Failure by Recipe

**The tiles in stucco marble that we made may be
very nice, but apparently they didn't turn out so well
technically. Aren't there any good recipes to follow?**
There is this thing about recipes. When I decided to learn
how to make stucco marble, I first followed the usual paths
to information—books, the Internet, friends—and eventually,
through our material archivist, this Bruno Lombardi
turned up, an absolute expert who had undertaken many
restorations of stucco marble. So I was able to learn this
technique from him in depth. Originally, he was supposed to
teach the workshop, but unfortunately he was sick. Bruno
collects all the books he can find on stucco marble, and
every recipe says something different. A slight change in the
plaster or the density of pigments can lead you to the point
where a recipe fails and becomes useless. In a way, you can
only teach how to get a feeling for the material. In the end,
only an experienced person can be a viable "recipe book"
for novices, by walking around, observing, and knowing
if you are filling the holes too wet or sanding too dry. This

requires an empathic attention, to recognize where the other person stands.

With your tiles you performed the essential procedures. What you didn't experience was the persistent patience needed for sanding just one grain finer, until new holes emerge, which you fill in again, and then sand just one grit finer until you reach 4000 grit. Doing it in three days, as we did, was too fast. If you were to make stucco marble for real, you would have to go at it every day or two for a month. Before you can even begin, you have to prepare the bone glue; the granulate has to be soaked two weeks in advance, then boiled. The glue, which delays the setting of the plaster, has to be mixed in a certain proportion to water, and then adjusted, so that the setting time falls between four and six hours. That requires several small experiments.

Couldn't one record all these experiences in the form of a recipe?

Of course you could explain any number of things, but it's impossible to account for all types of plasters, glues, and pigments. A recipe can only "quasi-teach" and can't ever incorporate every possibility of failure.

In the case of our tiles, the filling plaster apparently wasn't thick enough, actually a small mistake. In Bruno's opinion, however, the majority was not salvageable. There is an affectionate conflict between the two of us, that in my view you don't really need so much to succeed, and he, who is much more experienced, insists on what you can and cannot do. But if I had always abided by his rules,

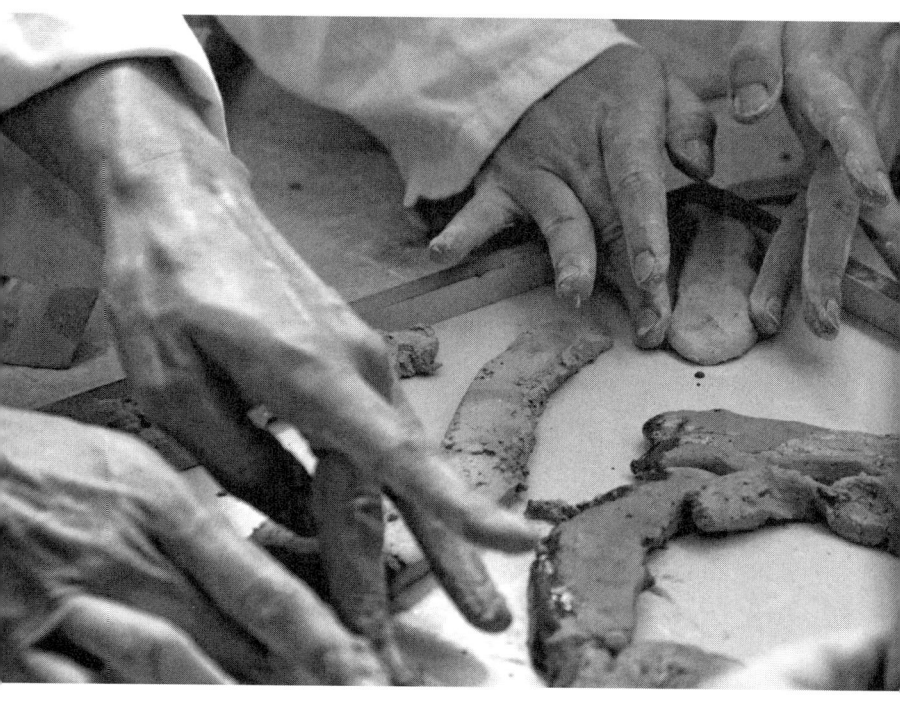

I would never have been able to realize my large works. I approached this adventure relatively fearlessly and with a certain impatience, and somehow it worked. I'm also greatly interested in getting chance on board, precisely by not knowing, and then watching how awesomely this chance plays out.

Felix Lehner

The Importance of Doing

How do you proceed when an artist wants to make a piece of art at the foundry at Sitterwerk?
Often an artist will come with a vague notion, and at first we listen patiently. The artistic idea often changes rapidly, and because of this, taking it seriously and being able to let it go are equally important in the process of developing the work. While you play with different ideas and variants of materials, you encounter resistances that are immanent to the material. In order to realize the artistic idea in the end, you have to overcome a certain number of these resistances.

It's impossible to plan this development in advance. Perhaps it's also the inability to think something through in a structured way; in any case, it is only through judging the result of an effort that one can evaluate whether it does justice to the artistic idea. The delight in working this way stems from the interplay of observing, contemplating, and doing, and not simply from planning theoretically. In a certain way, this can slow the process down, but sometimes it also totally accelerates it.

Do your raw materials come from a catalog, or do you have to produce them specifically for your purposes?

Both can occur. When working with standardized products, however, we've come to realize that believing in their unchanging composition is a complete illusion. Every plaster changes depending on where in the pit it was excavated. Regulations banning the use of certain toxic substances also affect the composition of a material. Some products that have been available for decades under the same name are slightly altered, and suddenly something doesn't work in the usual way. Thus, we continually have to test the performance of a particular product. Frequently the materials that we want to use are alien to the purpose, i.e., they are not intended for the application we envision. And often, the unfinished state of processing is much more interesting than the finished one. It is precisely these intermediate forms, which often aren't really paid attention to, that sometimes embody exactly the quality we've been seeking. We make a sample, try to achieve a reliable quality, and then it may happen that no one dares to make a judgment for a while. This brought about the idea of the material archive at Sitterwerk, where all the intermediate forms and their properties are recorded.

What forms of knowledge play a role?

I believe that diversity—our multifaceted interests and experiences—is really advantageous to our work. From the artist's perspective, it may sometimes be a disadvantage to pursue too many possibilities. I see an incredible value in an artist's narrow focus, and it is a pleasure to make our possibilities, our broad knowledge, and our wealth of experience available to support that. We have developed a highly diverse mix of professions here in the art foundry. Our capabilities now comprise not only the processing of wax, plaster, clay, cement, all minerals, metals, and wood for formwork, but also carbon and Kevlar fiber-reinforced plastics, and bitumen. We are, so to speak, a craftspeople's collective of stonemasons, carpenters, mechanics, programmers, graphic designers, art historians, and philosophers. I am thrilled that so many perspectives, capabilities, and qualities coexist here so closely. Therefore, it is also important to have the art library and an exhibition space so close to the melting furnace, so that these worlds may move closer to each other.

Marco Ganz

I Contend: Lobster Red!

Bijoy, Katalin, and Ruedi showed us three different approaches to color. How can you compare them?
In my view, the approaches differ in their definition of a problem. In the houses by Studio Mumbai, I see the floor tiles pigmented in red or green as answering to the hues of the wood used in that particular architecture. In Ruedi's case, color operates in a more subtle area, revolving around materials and their inherent colors. Stucco marble focuses instead on individual expression.

How are the results related to their respective philosophies?
In Bijoy's work, I see much effort in the production of samples and that he achieves a personal attitude to color only by comparing a great number of them. I'm sure that his first sample is acceptable, but you can only know that sample No. 27 is clearly better if you have judged fifty of them. Such decisions, of course, always depend on personal preferences, too.

How do you arrive at deciding, and knowing, that a particular color is right?

You try something out and begin to evaluate. In my case, the certainty that a color is right is based simply on doing many trials. As the American painter Shirley Jaffe aptly expressed it, "I choose my colors by what they do." In this sentence she expresses nothing other than that she herself is deciding what the colors actually do. It is a personal decision that may be subjectively understood, but it cannot be objectively proved. Colors can begin to function when they are assigned a mission. I see decisions related to color as contentions; when you paint a house red, you claim that this house must have precisely that shade of red. Of course, such a decision requires engagement with questions of color.

In the final round of discussion at the end of the workshop, you provocatively claimed that Switzerland has only a humble culture with regard to color, especially compared to India. What were you alluding to?

You see, we are a small country of farmers, and we never had a royal dynasty that cultivated the use of colors. If, on the other hand, the Vatican were in Zurich, if we had owned colonies, then we would certainly have a richer, more exotic, and more symbolically charged palette at our disposal. India, as well as England or France, boasts many famous and historically significant colors: Indian Yellow, British Racing Green, Chartreuse . . . . Switzerland just cannot keep up.

Perhaps the fear of using colors, which was brought up in the final round of discussion, is a result of this humble culture?

I suppose so. And the demonstrative overcoming of this fear, as seen from time to time in projects built by younger architecture firms, can lead to rather shrill results.

This would justify the fear of color, wouldn't it?

Exactly, we have to thank architects when they use colors with the necessary respect. The mere desire to make something colorful is insufficient; in using color, you have to be up to something.

Can color systems be of help here?

Theories communicate a deceptive sense of security. Nothing can relieve you of having to try things out, to examine and modify them again and again. For instance, the idea that a wall could be red or orange is worthless. However, to aspire toward the color of a cooked lobster, because you happen to be dealing with a seafood restaurant, is an infinitely more valuable approach. Suddenly you discover the hue that hits the nail on the head.

Salome Lippuner

Making Your Own Craft

Your use of the Japanese lacquer *urushi* is quite novel. How did it come about?

As a youth I had wanted to become an architect, in fact, but that didn't work out. Since I was eager to do something with my hands, I started by learning the goldsmith's craft. But space continued to interest me, and I also designed some furniture for my home. I encountered Japanese lacquer as a child and was fascinated by its wonderful sheen. After a minimal introduction to the lacquering craft, I began using *urushi* in my jewelry. On my first trip to Japan I saw these incredibly beautiful lacquered interiors, and an architect there, who showed an interest in my objects, brought me into contact with some artists who wanted to renew the art of lacquering. He then sent me back to Europe with recipes for the architectural application of lacquer.

You could count on support from Japan, but how did you discover your own personal way of working?

By necessity I had to discover it in Europe because, for one,

I couldn't have afforded the long training in Japan. On the other hand, this disadvantage met favorably with my need for freedom, because I did not want to subordinate myself to the Japanese canon. I wanted to acquire the craft of lacquering experimentally and free of prescribed models. Only in a second step, when I was in Japan again, did I become acquainted with working traditionally.

In Japan, you learn a craft through prolonged imitation of a master. The exercise dictates what something must look like when it is finished; you work with great exactitude. But along the way you hardly look at what is coming into being. I am a strong proponent of "right now" and of observing what is actually happening with an idea, your skill, and the material. Sometimes I also purposely make a mistake, which often sparks a discussion with my Japanese colleagues. This ongoing exchange across cultures is another important element in my work.

My pieces are crafted from a dialogue between mind, hand, and material; an ongoing shaping by and of experience. Intuition and dexterity reveal themselves through interplay, such as is the case with a musician or a dancer.

André Murer and René Odermatt

Venture and Faith

In your opinion, what sets Bijoy's working method apart?
ANDRÉ: It is interesting how Bijoy evades the standard
thinking that revolves around costs, deadlines, and liability.
His decision to work so closely with craftspeople from
the beginning overcomes the usual separation of design
and construction, brought about by the need for a bidding
process.
RENÉ: Yes, Bijoy certainly doesn't build the ordinary jobs. His
method of focusing so strongly on craft is highly individual,
and for me it is also the clear expression of the will to work
this way. And, naturally, the other side also has to be willing.

How do things continue from there?
ANDRÉ: You need an engagement of a certain intensity in
order to begin something. A mutual trust can then develop
between craftsperson and architect, and beyond that, to the
client as well. This trust subsequently permits pursuing one's
objectives more specifically.
RENÉ: The point is to gain know-how together, to make

teamwork and collaboration natural and self-evident. Knowledge always builds upon what has already been. Bijoy told us about the longstanding tradition of his artisans. Surely, that also strengthens his credibility.

How did you experience the encounter with craft in the workshop?

ANDRÉ: Normally, I imagine what something might look like at the beginning of a task. It was liberating, in the context of the workshop, to be able to try something out just for its own sake. You simply begin and you really look at what is happening in front of you. Usually it's the moments of decision that are full of suspense: do you really have the courage to do something the way you imagined? Or do you play it safe? In the workshop, we didn't really have any responsibility; we could experiment without prejudice and just see what happened.

RENÉ: What really interested me was something that only came up in the discussion on the last day, namely, experimenting and simultaneously failing. It takes courage to extend your willingness to fail farther and farther, up to the point where things get too hot for you. How much risk can you stand? At what point do you become conservative and follow a sure path? It's the question of how free you want to be, and Bijoy has trained himself very successfully to think freely.

Working with my hands has expanded my mental capacity in the sense that I've learned to pursue an idea in parallel with working haptically. I appreciated that Ruedi didn't lay out

theoretical rules for this in advance, but that he let us work for a week to attain this insight.

Ueli Vogt

Opening Up the Dialogue

What made Studio Mumbai an interesting subject for the exhibition at the material archive at Sitterwerk?

At first I thought Studio Mumbai was a collective system of craftspeople and designers creating something through dialogue. Only later I realized that a creative will was strongly at work there. Bijoy is deftly utilizing something that exists in India, and that is high-quality craftsmanship that doesn't cost much. He can examine all his designs in countless mock-ups.

Furthermore, he is a brilliant observer who makes short videos on his phone with a sharp eye—and not just of houses, but of daily life. And that flows into his architecture. Of course he noticed the quality of craftsmanship in India. His principle is clearly, "Take advantage of your opportunities."

What was important in curating this exhibition?

The exhibition in the material archive was intended to devote itself wholly to Bijoy's method and its artifacts. We set up the exhibition quite directly, sorting the material into three categories and laying it out according to groups of tools, material samples, and models. We also had these short films with a soundtrack where you could hear hammering and clanging, and then when you opened the door to the outside, you had the art foundry with its own hammering and clanging, sometimes produced by similarly archaic methods.

The term, "atmosphere," is, I believe, key to this coalescence. For example, it was also essential that Bijoy didn't just come to lecture on his techniques, but that in the end he went home having learned a great deal himself. The workshop was thus an integral part of the exhibition; without it, the exhibition wouldn't really have interested me.

What in all this fascinates us in Switzerland?
It's probably a kind of longing for endless details and those elaborate joints. We are subject to many more constraints here. A window catalog has perhaps thirty different windows to choose from; I think Bijoy starts with thirty different window mock-ups made to his taste.

There exist different depths of focus, in a way, and in Bijoy's case, the depth is virtually infinite. He can define every nail; I suppose he even requires that all screws be aligned in a certain direction because that is important to him. Here you have to make do with a different depth of engagement.

Is that to be regretted in every respect?
In a certain way, my understanding of what Bijoy does is still a bit vague. The production of models and mock-ups appears very impressive, but here, façade samples of larger

buildings are also built at 1:1 scale. But when Bijoy does that for a single-family home, we perceive it as sensational.

I think in the end, the quality of his approach is reflected most strongly in the way the projects occupy the site, when they sprinkle the sawdust on the ground and place the models into the context. I just find it incredibly beautiful how his houses sit in the landscape.

Could you apply some of this in Switzerland?

We have been asking ourselves how you could build with Bijoy's approach in Switzerland, and I have the feeling that the knowledge of how they forge iron in India, for example, is not that significant. I also think Bijoy would build in a completely different way here; he would take advantage of something specific that we have here, for example our well-developed building industry. I imagine he would even build with windows made from plastic; he would demonstrate a more open spirit than we would.

While here, for instance, he observed that we mark out planned buildings with poles on site before they are built. You don't find this practice in Germany—not to mention anything about the United States—that you simulate a building at 1:1 scale. It goes in the direction of what he does: a simulated house. However, we do it only so that the neighbors can see if they'll still be able to see anything after the structure is built. If I were to build here with Bijoy, I would like to use the markers as a design tool—those markers as the first part of a construction—and see how the house takes shape from there.

What are the advantages with which you would be able to win support for this procedure from the authorities?

There are an endless number of regulations, but despite them, the resulting buildings and spaces often do not turn out well. If a project were able to develop in an iterative process instead of in the rigid sequence that is usually followed, that could be a first step. Perhaps you erect an illegal structure first and get the permit after. Or you promise that you'll do a good job. Or, first you get a permit for the construction markers, and then the rest would just be alteration permits. We should really try that!

Recipes

Mixing Fire Clay and Plaster

Fire clay, a waste product of the foundry process at Sitterwerk, is mixed with plaster and water in varying proportions and applied to a wetted cement tile with a trowel. Layer after layer is applied. Working each layer into the previous one strengthens the bond between them. Different tools of application leave a characteristic trace. Ground earth pigments can be worked into the surface before it hardens. (Bijoy Jain)

Three Ways of Quenching Lime

1) QUENCHING THE LIME BY OVERSATURATION: Thoroughly mix approximately 2.5 parts water with 1 part burnt lime; the result is pit lime, which is then stored for several years in tanks or pits before use. Natural settling of the material creates layers of differing quality, which, depending on grain size, are used for paintwork, fine plaster finishings, or mortar. Fine pit lime, diluted into a slurry, can be used to bind pigments.

2) RESTRAINED QUENCHING OF LIME: By adding too little water (1 part water to 2 parts burnt lime), the lime crumbles into a coarse powder in the course of a few days. Mixing it with water again (1 part water to 3–4 parts lime) produces a spreadable paste, which can be applied as a plaster for compacted or polished surfaces.

3) DRY QUENCHING: Layer sand and quicklime (in the proportion of 3:1) into a box with a permeable bottom and flood it with water. The reaction of the lime with the water produces steam that permeates the pile. Excess water seeps out. After a few days, one can cut away portions vertically and mix them into a mortar or wall plaster.
(Ruedi Krebs)

Stucco Marble

Combine alabaster or modeling plaster, mixed with a maximum of 5 % pigment (which has to be light-fast and lime-resistant), with water and bone glue (from granulate). Form flat strips of different colors. Fold the strips over each other to form a loaf with differently colored veins; cut into slices about 1.5 cm thick. Lay out the still wet slices face down on a board or glass plate lubricated with Vaseline. Fill in the remaining spaces with plaster in a single color.

After the plate has hardened, sand the flat face with a 200 grit sanding block; sponge continuously. Tiny air enclosures will come to the surface as it is sanded. Fill them in firmly with the same plaster/pigment/water/bone glue mixture. At an interval of one or two days (when the filling has hardened),

continue with a finer sanding block and fill in the emerging holes until a 4000 grit is reached.
(Katalin Deér)

Wood Frame Wall Mock-Up

Build a timber frame with a latticework of evenly spaced wooden slats or willow branches on the inside. Cover the lattice joints in clay. Apply a mortar of lime recipe No. 2, mixed with hemp fibers, to the lattice and gradually fill the frame until the width of the wood is reached. The surface can be finished with a variety of tools or by hand.
(Bijoy Jain and Ruedi Krebs)

Kheer (Indian Milk Rice)

1 part rice
10 parts milk
Cardamom powder, saffron
½ part sugar
Boil milk with cardamom and saffron. Soak rice in water for 10 minutes. Drain rice and add to milk. When hot, add sugar. Cook slowly until all the liquid is absorbed.
(Priya Jain)

Biographies

Katalin Deér

Katalin Deér, born in 1965 in Palo Alto, California, is an artist working with photography and sculpture. She lives in St. Gallen. In 2011, she completed a public art project in Arbon, with stucco marble and photographs cast in exposed concrete (with Meier Hug Architects, Zurich).

Marco Ganz

Marco Ganz, born in 1961, works and lives in Zurich. Originally a graphic and font designer, he has been a freelance artist since 1993. With a focus on sculpture, he specializes in new materials and production methods. Since 2009, he has produced several editions dealing explicitly with color.
www.marcoganz.ch
www.colorbeautycase.ch

Bijoy Jain

Bijoy Jain was born in Mumbai, India in 1965 and received his M.Arch from Washington University in St. Louis, Missouri, in

1990. He worked in Los Angeles and London between 1989 and 1995 and returned to India in 1995 to found his practice.

The work of Studio Mumbai has been presented in many exhibitions, including the XII Venice Biennale and at the Victoria & Albert Museum. Bijoy Jain and Studio Mumbai have received many awards, including the Global Award in Sustainable Architecture (2009); recognition as a finalist in the 11th cycle of the Aga Khan Award for Architecture (2010); the Spirit of Nature Wood Architecture Award, Finland (2012); the BSI Swiss Architecture Award (2012); and, most recently, the Grande Medaille d'Or from the Academie D'Architecture, Paris, France (2014). In 2014, the University of Hasselt, Belgium, bestowed an honorary doctorate on Jain.

Ruedi Krebs

Born in 1956, Ruedi Krebs first apprenticed as a stonemason and spent his travel years in France and Germany. He has been running his own shop since 1983. Since 1986, his research has made him a specialist for construction techniques with lime, including lime plaster floors. He was a lecturer for materials at Fachklasse für Innenarchitektur FFI (now Academy of Art and Design at the University of Applied Sciences and Arts Northwestern Switzerland) in Basel, Switzerland, from 1990 to 1998. He lives in Twann, Switzerland.

Felix Lehner

Felix Lehner was born in St. Gallen in 1960. After an apprenticeship as a bookseller, he began casting art and established the art foundry in Beinwil am See in 1983,

which transferred to St. Gallen in 1994, where it has been expanding continually under his supervision. He established the Sitterwerk Foundation in 2006, along with Daniel Rohner and Hans Jörg Schmid. Since 2007, he has been setting up a branch of the foundry in Shanghai.
www.kunstgiesserei.ch

Salome Lippuner

Salome Lippuner, born in 1956, apprenticed as a goldsmith, and later studied in Zurich and Wajima, Japan. She received a scholarship for a residency at the Cité Internationale des Arts in Paris in 2012–2013. She was a lecturer for design at Lehrgang für praktische Denkmalpflege in Laas, Italy, and in Krems, Austria. She has been running her independent studio since 1986. She lives and works in Twann, Switzerland.
www.urushi.ch

Hubert Mäder

Hubert Mäder studied architecture at ETH Zurich and spent an exchange semester in Ahmedabad, India. He is in charge of public events and international exchange at Zurich University of Applied Sciences in Winterthur, Switzerland.
www.archbau.zhaw.ch

André Murer

André Murer is a learnt draftsman and studied architecture at Lucerne University of Applied Arts and Sciences. He worked for Ai Weiwei in Beijing and Cometti Truffer Architekten in Lucerne. Following the workshop at Sitterwerk, he spent six

months at Studio Mumbai. Since 2013, he has been a partner at MAI Architekten in Lucerne.
www.maiarchitektur.ch

René Odermatt

René Odermatt is a wood sculptor and artist. He directs the workshops for casting, forming, and carving objects in a variety of techniques and materials at the School for Art and Design at Lucerne University of Applied Arts and Sciences.
www.reneodermatt.ch

Samuel P. Smith

Samuel P. Smith, born in 1981 and raised in Basel, studied music at Yale University and architecture at ETH Zurich. He has interned at architecture firms in New York, Buenos Aires, Zurich, and Tokyo, and worked for Peter Zumthor from 2012 to 2014. In 2014, he started his own practice.
www.samuel-smith.com

Ueli Vogt

Ueli Vogt, born in 1965, apprenticed as a landscape gardener and studied architecture at Zurich University of Applied Sciences, Winterthur. He was director of the material archive at Sitterwerk from 2008 to 2011. Since 2011, he has worked as a curator at Zeughaus Teufen, including the Grubenmann Museum.

• • •

ETH Zurich

ETH Zurich is one of the leading international universities for technology and the natural sciences. Its Department of Architecture is one of the most highly regarded faculties of architecture in the world. The architectural education owes its success to the fruitful intertwining of the teaching staff's academic instruction and practical building activity.
www.ethz.ch, www.arch.ethz.ch

Sitterwerk

On the industrial area in the Sittertal near St. Gallen, artists, craftspeople, scientists, and a broad public meet. The Sitterwerk, with its art library, material archive, and studio house, and the Kesselhaus Josephsohn Gallery, forms the institutional center among a network of producers of art and cultural-entrepreneurial enterprises. In the art foundry, photo lab, book workshop, and other institutions of the Sitterwerk, the production, research, conservation, presentation, and mediation of art interfuse and enrich one another in a multifaceted manner.
www.sitterwerk.ch

Studio Mumbai

Founded by Bijoy Jain, Studio Mumbai works with a human infrastructure of skilled artisans, technicians, and draftsmen, who design and build the work directly. This group shares an environment created from an iterative process, where ideas are explored through the production of large-scale

mock-ups, models, material studies, sketches, and drawings. Projects are developed through a careful consideration of place and practice that draws from traditional skills, local building techniques, materials, and an ingenuity arising from limited resources.
www.studiomumbai.com